www.finishinglinepress.com

Blame It
on the Serpent

poems by

Susan Vespoli

Finishing Line Press
Georgetown, Kentucky

Blame It
on the Serpent

Profits from *Blame It on the Serpent*
will be donated
to addiction recovery groups:

P.A.L. (Parents of Addicted Loved Ones,)
Al-Anon,
ACOA (Adult Children of Alcoholics
& Dysfunctional Families,)
and others.

Publisher: Leah Huete de Maines
Editor: Christen Kincaid
Cover Art: Marina Petra's painting *Serpent Descending*
Author Photo: Marianne Killick
Cover Design: Elizabeth Maines McCleavy

Order online: www.finishinglinepress.com
also available on amazon.com

Author inquiries and mail orders:
Finishing Line Press
P. O. Box 1626
Georgetown, Kentucky 40324
U. S. A.

Table of Contents

IV.

*For my kids, grandkids,
teachers, & all the 12-Step groups
on the planet*

I.

I mean, you love them so much you would throw yourself
in front of an incoming missile to protect them.
They with their innocence and soft skin.
They who know not what dangers
lurk in the belly of the world.

Let Go

Unclasp hands
from mine
brush palms
I watch them
tumble
into darkness
I know not
where they land

Chicken

"I didn't cause it, can't control it, can't cure it." ~Al-Anon slogan

I tried to write a poem
about how the opioid epidemic
had stolen one of my children,
now an adult,
and how it threatens
like a terrorist
to take another,
about how there's nothing
a mother can do but watch
the way a body thins, how teeth dissolve,
how beings disappear
from behind their own eyes:
the brown or green irises darkening,
the eyeballs resting
in more hollow sockets—
but the words, lines, stanzas
of my poem attempts
were all failures.

So, instead I will tell about a golden hen
that appeared in my backyard
like magic
to stand on her four-prong-star feet,
her body an oval covered with feathers
a strawberry blond fluffy as fur
backlit by the sun
when she bent to sip water
from the pale green bowl
I'd placed beneath the Palo Verde tree.
At first she strutted like a little queen
around the center of the grassy expanse
surrounded by oleanders,
sort of haughty, wide-eyed, solo,
but then she began to trust me,
sidling up to my ankles,

saying *bwak, bwak, bwak*
like she had some news to share
and I grew to sort of love her.
Then one day, as it happens,
I looked for her and she was gone.

Bless the Bee

Bless the baby with skin so sensitive
contact can feel like abrasion
and bless the mother who cuts the feet

from sleepers, clips neck-tags from shirts,
and buys only seamless socks.
Bless the teen who hides

Ziploc-bagged drugs in his dresser
found by the mother
next to cardboard bongs

made from toilet-paper tubes, tin foil,
and flat packs of rolling papers
she hauls to the curb and throws away.

Bless the car ride when he tells her nothing
feels better than being stoned
and he will never quit

so she watches his eyes
stay glassy from pot or pills
or powder to blur the world.

Bless the man so afraid of needles;
she knows he will never shoot up.
Today, the man is thinner,

not so often heard from,
wears a stained shirt,
says, *I'm fine, Mom,*

without really looking at her
until a bee buzzes onto her blouse
and he gasps, swats it

with his bare hand, kills

the fuzzy being, says
It almost stung you,
even stunning himself.

Saint Mom

I like to think of myself as a saint,
Mother Teresa reborn as a blond.

I like to think of myself with a halo
of light, my arms

circling a baby I've calmed
with a lullaby. But I've been told

that my words can be razor-
blades, sharp enough to draw blood

and I don't believe this

until my kids mimic
my, "What an asshole," at their father

or spit, "Shit!" from their car seats
at drivers who cut me off

or that time my 13-year-old carried
an audio recorder in his pocket, needling

me till I snapped, "Goddam it, NO!"
Then played it back to me as blackmail.

After Toilet Training her Brother

I wasn't going to even try
with my daughter until she was two,
but I bought a potty chair

and she figured it out—
left surprise bowls of yellow
liquid or black pearls.

Her brother was hard to train
because he wouldn't do
anything I wanted him to do,

which is pretty funny now
when I think about it.
Instead of peeing in toilets,

he'd drop his pants in the front yard
and water the annuals,
shrubbery, evergreens.

Once, he stood in the living room,
peed into his Little Tikes wagon,
grinning as I came down the stairs.

I threw the vehicle over
my head and into the garage—
but didn't scold.

I wasn't supposed
to show anger
while training.

Backyard Pool – Phoenix 1995

Your not-yet-ex husband
crashes on the couch

after another beer, another bout
of contempt, dishwasher loaded,

pans scrubbed, counters freed
of crumbs. There's nothing left

to do but squeeze the sponge,
turn off the faucet, and walk

out the sliding glass door
into the yard, past lawn chairs,

the kids' pool noodles, goggles.
You climb up and step to the end

of the diving board, hover over
the water in your T-shirt and jeans,

your children startled from their T.V. show
to ask, *Mom, where are you going?*

You, usually too busy
with who knows what to play or swim
are now drawn to the cool blue
rectangle, to be weightless,

swallowed by a whoosh
that mutes the world.

I Come from a Line of Women

Named after saints, queens,
and mothers of Jesus
who knit pictures into sweaters,
channel Ouija boards into books,
and defecate into cranberry boxes
while on road trips by themselves.

I come from a line of women
who glue false eyelashes
onto their lids in their eighties,
sport jungle pelt prints,
and wallpaper bathrooms
with photos of Tom Jones.

I come from a line of women
who drag children cross country by train
to locate philandering husbands
and say meals must contain a root,
leaf, and seed vegetable.

I come from a line of women
who fly Beechcrafts, lead Girl Scouts,
travel the world and say they will
only come home in a box.

I come from a line of women
who drop dead outside of parked cars
still holding the keys in their hands.

November Late Afternoon, 2005

Out of the McMansion on the hill, I drove fast,
followed the U-Haul truck driven by my friend
who helped me move the few things I'd need
to survive. I left the 3-car garage, the triple-digit
income, the Visa bills of gambling, strippers,
and booze. I brought my antique dresser,
the round maple table I ate on as a kid, a loveseat,
all my clothes, the cheapest new bed I could find,
mismatched dishes, pots, pans, and towels
from Goodwill, and felt like a millionairess
who'd just discovered a new light-filled world.

II.

And with all your vigilant amoxycillin, gate locks, sleuthing,
and samurai seatbelt moves, they'll still lie semi-conscious in a hospital
with meningitis. They'll become injured in a mysterious
daycare accident and end up deaf in one ear. You have not had time
to realize the extent of some humans' damage.
This will be the first lesson that your kids want for you,
to know you will need to learn this.

My Son No Longer Missing

I like to think he graduated
from the methadone clinic,
now does yoga, gave up

smoking. I like to think he grew
a new set of bright teeth
to replace the ones that rotted.

I like to think he rents a studio
with a patio near the canal
filled with crappies and sunfish

not nodding off with homeless junkies.
I like to think he leans back
in an Adirondack, after loading

the dishwasher with cupcake pans
from birthday muffins like the ones
he baked for me topped with candles

that he brought to the Mex place
where he hired a trio of sequined
mariachis to serenade us

as we dined on cheese enchiladas.
I like to think he is waiting
for just the right minute of the right hour

of the right day to reappear

        to tell me he is living

free of pills and booze and meth
and smack and at the end
of each long hot Phoenix day,

he drops himself
into the cool blue complex pool,
then emerges shiny, dripping.

13

3 AM Sonnet

A woman worries, grieves inside my head,
she's quiet as I go about my day.
Don't listen, I scold myself and go to bed.
You're strong, so knock it off, don't be afraid.

But then, asleep, it comes again: the dream.
I'm standing on a shore, some beach at night
and see my daughter floating out to sea.
I scream her name, she's silent, drifts from sight.

Her non-response sends chills, my heartbeats freeze.
She's twenty-two, tattooed, and bright, too sexy.
Daily pills from shrinks have dosed her needs.
Who needs Mama's phone calls or her texts?

I bolt awake at 3AM with dread
to hear her crying, the woman in my head.

To survive summer on the street

squat beneath shade trees
Sleep on a park bench

in the oleanders
behind a stoplight on Central.

Wake up, stretch
your arms above your head,

lean way back and release
an audible yawn.

Stash your bedroll in the shadows,
pace like a trapped cat

before settling on the spot to hold
your sign so high cars can't miss it.

Say thank you for every dollar
through sunburnt lips.

Wear your hair like Jesus
and sing to invisible friends.

Zigzag

Logo of a man's face
on a flat pack of rolling papers,
tea leaves sprinkle fortunes
too loosely, seams come undone
even when licked,

the end lit with a flicked match.
In and out of spicy smoke,
seeds pop, munchies
mix with paranoia.
He disappears into clouds
like Birdman.

Burning Coal

He was clean, thin, older, wore camouflage
patterned running shoes a size larger
than his feet. Knee length shorts,
a tee-shirt bearing the word DOPE
in caps above a graphic of a diamond

and his teeth reminded me of press-on nails
and the new wrinkles around his eyes
and his eyes themselves had become his dad's
eyes only kinder. And he talked about karma
and had found god on the street

in those he shared water with or bummed
cigarettes from, who said no one had ever been
so kind to them. And I said you know I love
you and think of you every day and he smiled
and nodded his bald head that seemed

so different from the last time I saw it
and I decided that yes, he looks almost
like Gandhi now and maybe Gandhi's mother
carried her son around in her chest
like a burning coal, too.

Rise and Fall

The Roman Empire. The price of gas.
A glass elevator in a high-rise.
The white Mohawk of waves
continually parting the blue. Surfers
in their slick black suits viewed
from a pier. A fake fur raccoon
tossed into the air by my dog.
A diving board of pigeons facing south
on a streetlamp. Alternating legs
of the cloud-haired jogger as he floats
past my window every morning. Cosmos
buds flying from the top of their stems
like helium balloons, like pursed lips,
like fists, opening to drop petals
on the dirt. My hopes for a brilliant addict,
his weight plummeting on a scale, his voice
saying he's just tired. The pill to his lips.
The gravedigger's shovel. A siren wailing
through the morning like a messenger.

Alex's Teeth

(Spiraling Abecedarian)

Alex's
bottom
crept up like
Duo of
emerging
finial twins
grinders
held
innocence
jammed beneath pillow.
kissed up to tooth fairy
Lots."   The
(me)
"No"
only rarely.
pillow, smiled
quilt.   No sign of
Really
sans orthodontia.
to die for eventually
ugly. I can't watch them
vanishing into
wasting gray.
Rx. Then junk.
him dissolve,
zilch. Zot.

baby
choppers
darts.
early pearls
front row
grinners
happy sprouts
in mouth like
jiggled loose, lost,
Kid notes
"Leave cash, please.
mom
never said
or maybe
Put five bucks under his
quietly smoothed
rotting then. Cavity free.
straight
Teeth
under siege. Addiction is
vanquished,
white powder,
Xed out by OxyContin
Ya. I can't watch
zero each enamel bead into

Why I Go to Al-Anon

~for my daughter

The bird was tiny, a sparrow
or rock wren, a brown-gray ball
of flittering feathers smacking
herself from one mesh window
into another on my screen porch
in what I thought was an attempt
to get out. She was stuck,

so, I moved to save her,
opened the door and swooshed
her like an aircraft marshaller
on the tarmac waving directions:
this way! this way! but she didn't
get it, so I grabbed a broom
and swept the air like I was wind—

created movement to force her
to stop slamming herself against
unopenable windows and finally
she woke up, lifted off walls,
winged toward daylight,
toward forest and as she flew
I felt like the bodhisattva of birds,

releasing her, easing suffering
and as she crossed through the portal
into what I viewed as her saved life,
out of the shadows, leaped my dog,
who looks like that Life-Is-Good
dog on coffee mugs and tee-shirts,
coming after her with canine-

teeth-wolf-jaws wide open
and because this is the nature
of the beast, my dog caught her

in one swoop, then swallowed,
and I in my 5-foot-3 body stood
beneath the 100-foot Ponderosa
pines and cried.

Even Bodhisattvas Get the Blues

Pema Chodron, a Buddhist nun
who teaches peace and compassion worldwide,

once threw a rock at the forehead
of her former husband—

which gives me hope.

Even though I meditate,
listen to self-help CDs,

mediate conflicts at work,
where a large, carved BE HAPPY sign
hangs above my desk,

at home I still roll my eyes,
slam doors, and pepper
my sentences with the word *fuck.*

And when you, oh love of my life,
say that after all your years of training as a therapist,

you *certainly* know how to communicate
with me, who reminds you of a wet cat,

I can't help but snap:
Well, your skills still suck with me,

the middle finger of my voice
rising like a whack-a-mole.

Bagged

"You didn't bother to tell me before I drove two-and-a-half hours to visit?" ~Me

How'd he quit the relationship?
By removing gold ring from his left finger.
Susie-Sunshine-Can-Be-Stupid
asks, "Where's your ring?"
"Stopped wearing it," his terse reply
while taking another bite of salad.
"Too little time together." Utterly
nonchalant with an especially passive
undertone of violence. Or was that me
who wanted to smash that glass
Buddha head into my now X's noggin,
a man still forking fish from plate
to mouth, a man who X-ed me out
after X number of years
without even mentioning it?

All his clothes and shoes bagged
in Hefty black plastic. Closet emptied
and wiped down of his smell, like after
a death, except he's still breathing
up in Flagstaff. Fucker used to be
a good word, not a slur. "Pour
your hormone replacement
purple ovals into the trash
and you won't miss him," jokes
my friend, like it's estrogen,
not his kiss, voice, fingertips
that used to trip the lust switch.
Men! Who needs 'em?
Loser. (Me or him?)

III.

I wear a white dress
made by Gunne Sax. When the minister says,
"Repeat after me,"
I can't remember the words.

Sleeping

While I was sleeping, my oldest son
grew a bushy gray beard and shaved his head.

While I was sleeping, the other two who I breastfed
for 15 and 18 months started smoking in their teens

and what that says about my nipples, I can't say.
While I was sleeping, people pitched dome tents

outside the ferry exit ramp in Seattle. One guy
sat on an upended barrel and when I met his eyes

they scared me a little: so hard, blank, empty
like dirt clods or iron and I wondered what he'd seen

to turn them into such unlit thuds. He sold throwaway
newspapers with the headline "Fragile"

and I thought, isn't that the truth. I didn't want to judge
him, wanted to look again and see the little boy

or husband or father or nephew or baby he'd been,
loved by someone, held and rocked till he was sleeping.

Metaphor from the Gods

Thanksgiving weekend is the anniversary
of me leaving my ex-husband
who tried to talk me out of it by buying

flowers and taking me to dinner at Taste of Thai,
to drone about our future over yellow curry
and Singhas, as I sunk deeper

into the vinyl of my chair
and wondered if that was sewage
I was smelling, when a man came out

of the women's restroom, a plastic bucket
and plunger in his rubber-gloved hands. I knew
it was time to cut the crap and move on.

Decades After Marrying an Addict

You'll wind up here
sitting in a circle of chairs
with other parents of addicts
at a church you don't attend.

You'll all wear nametags,
forced smiles, bow your heads
as a prayer is said, and then
take turns telling tales

of kids in prison, rehab,
psych wards, kids on meth,
on oxy, heroin, Xanax, acid,
of the grandkids some are raising

and you won't crack
when you speak
of your own hooked kid

until the woman on your left
tells of the unexpected death
of her alcoholic husband,
the police knocking

at her door for her son,
her shoulders shaking, her sobbing,
"I'm scared," into her hands
and that's when you'll break down, too.

Descending, 2006 -1973

My daughter makes popcorn in my new apartment while I'm at work. Neighbors
    loan her their fire extinguisher. The walls turn gray.

We pass a body of water planned by landscape architects. I ask about the $500
    Sugar Cabaret charge on our AMEX card. The fountain water sprays into
    the air.

Our daughter wears a miniskirt and platform shoes. At the emergency room, she
    tries to kiss a gray bearded biker who she thinks is Neale Donald Walsch.

We are in a 5-star restaurant with the entourage of the governor. He orders another
    bottle of wine and I am in the elevator, descending.

I throw out our leather sectional because it smells like cat pee.

Our son shaves off his eyebrows, cuts his hair into a double Mohawk, and spray
    paints graffiti on his bedroom walls. He is taking drum lessons.

I make jelly from the fallen peaches in our yard.

I bake a Duncan Hines cake and top it with plastic Ninja Turtles.

My mother-in-law is thrown off a plane bound for Hawaii. Too much wine
    in the airport bar.

The stick dipped into urine says yes. I walk back to the bed. He
    says, "I'm happy for you."

We're in a restaurant visiting family in California. My mother-in-law screams
    at my husband. The other diners stare as he shrinks in his chair.

His godmother tells me the secret to a good spaghetti sauce is pork. "Sausage is
    best," she says, "but a pork chop will do."

My new mother-in-law smashes every glass jar from her fridge into the kitchen
    sink. Her wine bottle is empty.

I walk through the glass doors of Lucky's Grocery Store carrying my
toddler on a hip. He says, "Come through my line," wearing his nametag on
an apron. I wonder if Vespoli is Greek.

I throw up every morning and my mother takes up golf. We live on Guam.

How to Celebrate your Daughter's 33rd Birthday when There's No Going Back

Go south and then west to a distant unknown
address. Drive past junk yards, steel shops, stacked
car parts, and a billboard for weed pizza. Breathe.

Remember the last time you saw her, Christmas,
and before that, the car ride between hospital stays.
Bring the cake you baked, the kind she likes: cocoa frosted

yellow square plus cupcakes left at home for her daughter.
Pack the gift bag, pink tissue-papered things she asked for:
track phone, cleansers in a plastic tub, socks. Card you made

from an old photo, your arms circling her little-
girl body, both of you smiling, her grin with perfect
rows of baby teeth, yours in plum lipstick. Park, watch

her walk to your car, barefoot, no pants, long red tee-shirt,
dark hair coiling to her waist. Wave. Say hi, make eye
contact. Hand her envelopes, bags, the tin pan

of golden cake. Hear her say *thank you*. Follow her
through the front door into a house with no furniture.
Learn the boyfriend you don't know is upstairs. Ask

if she's taking care of herself. Listen to the wind howl.
See her eyes dance backward. Worry. Swirling
dust outside the window. Look how she opens

the card, finds a trace of who you two were then
is still here in this empty unfamiliar room. Put your arms
around her, feel her wobble. Say, *enjoy your cake*! Wonder
if there's any chance they even have a knife.

Blame it on the Serpent

"Addiction is sneaky, it slithers in." ~Anonymous

I managed the whole world
        back then, so a lot on my plate:
                the seasons, stars, moon, plants, and animals.

I figured Adam and Eve
        would blossom
                in that garden of paradise.

But no. First it was the forbidden apple,
        then gambling trips to Vegas
                in his Cadillac, then strip clubs, a pool table

in the living room, fully stocked house bar
        open 24/7, Red Bulls and bongs,
                overflowing ashtrays

and then notes from the serpent asking Adam to score.
        "Don't tell your mother,"
                he'd scribbled on one.

Sin, sin, sin all over creation.
        Did they think I wouldn't see them?
                Goddam serpent.

Wedding Party

"It is essential to tell the truth at all times." ~John Bradshaw

A raisin dropped in a glass
of champagne will bounce
up and down for hours,
which explains my daughter's wedding:

>   pickled partiers in tight black gowns,
>   suits, the unexpected downpour
>   that moves the ceremony indoors.

My daughter's face painted
a Lalo Cota mural off Central,
her groom's beard a bushy ZZ Top,
slur their vows with love,

>   wobble like Day-of-the-Dead
>   skeleton-couple cake-topper
>   in white icing atop their 3-tier.

Balloons strung from the ceiling
bop to the beat.
Guests grind, hips swivel
around the dance floor.

>   The maid of honor lifts her flute
>   in a toast filled with affectionate F-bombs.
>   Even my NASA-engineer sister throws back

Jell-O shots as my elder sister twerks,
while I, in my black dress and fishnets,
hold the newlyweds' baby,
swaying her, silently reciting

>   the Al-Anon Serenity Prayer,
>   *accept the things I cannot change,*
>   watch everyone revel and throb

except my parents who sit upright,
lips set in tight lines
to hold in whatever words
knock behind their teeth.

After the Divorce

After flying in a yellow plane
to the San Diego Airport,
you will stand on a curb
with a backpack and pup tent
and wait with people you know
by their calm and open faces
are going to the same place,
a monastery where a festival
of one-thousand people will coil
in long lines at bathrooms
and the dining hall and rattlesnakes
will crawl through the women's campground,
after you vow to be silent for five days,
and then the rains will come
as gentle finger taps, then cymbals
and drums, and the valleys and hills
will go gray to match the sky,
and when you wake at 6 a.m. to the sound
of a nun singing and ringing a deep gong,
you will rise to walk with a throng of meditators
led by a Vietnamese monk who you will never see,
but you will be swallowed by a stillness,
like diving underwater to swim the length
of a pool, a quiet so loud it throbs.

Ring Finger

The tip of my thumb
still reaches across

my palm's life line, heart
line, head line, stretches

over the Girdle of Venus
to touch the tender

base of Apollo, circling it,
surprised by the absence

of the glittery band, although
it's been gone for months.

Circumference of skin
still stunned to be naked

of the symbol, bauble, ballast,
zirconium disco ball,

although a rash rippled
the derma when I wore it,

pink bumps that prickled
into what I now see

were red flags.

IV.

You will be among those standing around the laboring
young mother-to-be as she prepares to give birth.
The morning sun will stream into the room
and someone will say, "Push,"
and she will.

I Dream of Him Somersaulting Underwater

Spiraling, smiling
young boy as whirligig
swimsuit-clad acrobat
blue backyard pool

I want to bottle him
pre-oxycontin script
playful, athletic kid:
tender tadpole.

Sonogram

When my daughter was a toddler
she stroked my cheek like it was the silk
edge of a blanket and pressed
the nipple-ends of soft balloons
into the plastic mouths of dolls

and when she grew breasts
boys flocked around her
like birds to our backyard
come to pluck seeds
from the center of a sunflower

and then her hands gained skill
to text friends, flick cigarettes
from the back porch, play *Bad Fish*
on guitar strings, and flip her middle
finger into the air like a slim bomb

until it finally folded back up, resting
in the cupped palm of the woman
who smiles at me from an exam table
with her eyes as bright as a camera flash
at the blip, blip, blip of a lit star that will be Molly.

Haiku for Missing my Granddaughter

I'm five states away
from she who twirls in socks, asks:
wanna dance with me?

Hoarding Light

I'm hoarding Molly
while on lockdown, luminescent
in her fourth year around the sun.

People gasp and ask,
you're still seeing your granddaughter?
like I'm committing a crime,

and I want to hide her behind my skirts.
She who chalks cement
with hearts, water-paints rocks,

watches youtube
compilations of Snoopy laughing
and never tires of tossing

the rubber bone to my ecstatic dog.
I turn off daily death counts on the news
to see her in the field of brilliant

poppies that sprang up in my front yard.
She who bends to sniff and pluck
and count the bees,

then runs after bugs
she wants to keep as pets:
crane flies and beetles,

a fat khaki grasshopper
wriggling between index finger
and her thumb,

as I the buzz-kill cry,
*It's a living being
that needs its family. Let it go,*

and she does: opens pincer grip
as the insect soars
across the yard in an arc.

In the Face of My Hospitalized Daughter (Molly's Mother), a Pandemic, a Relationship Breakup, and Political Turmoil: My House

~an abecedarian

A mountain reclines
behind my house, freckled with
cactus: saguaro, prickly pear, ocotillo on
dirt. *There it is!* She always points out the peak
enroute from her car seat, looks for it like a
friend that grows larger the closer we
get to what she's grown to call "our
house." A modest place where she
immediately removes her shoes, is
jumped on by two fur
kids, face-lickers, tail-waggers,
lovers of everything, especially
Molly who will then
nestle in to sketch
on a million sheets of
paper—portraits of herself, me, and them. Our
quartet in her art always smiling amidst
randomly placed hearts, flowers, rainbows, and that
same sun I drew as a kid, a fried egg
tucked up in the corner
under carefully crayoned caps of her name.
Vinca still blooms, survives in clay pots on the porch
while the hottest Phoenix summer on record tops
X number of degrees outside our AC bubble and
yum, we still bake peanut butter cookies, still
zigzag the top of each dough ball with a fork.

Ash

He seems taller. Thin, but not skinny. His T-shirt is clean. Gray. He strides in from another room like it hasn't been a year since I've seen him. Since I said I wouldn't give him money, and would he *please* go to treatment. Since he told me I deserted him along with his dad when I left.

*

I open my arms and he walks into them. An awkward hug, but still. The top of his scalp shines and is surrounded by a close wreath of stubble.

   I like your hair like that.

   What hair? his dad eavesdrops, snorts. He doesn't have any hair. Male pattern baldness comes from the maternal side.

   It looks good, I say. *I might cut mine like that.*

Alex's girlfriend's 5'6" frame is 90 pounds velveted in honey-gold skin. Its luster surprises me. There's a black hole in her gum where her incisor once lived.

*

I ask them about their cat.

   He's living in the bathroom. Wanna see him?

The black and gray tabby curls in the sink and looks up at me. Its fur stands up along its spine like a blade. I watch us in the mirror above the vanity. Alex smiles with teeth now the color of ash.

In A Booth with a 3-Year Old

Let me tell you how Molly
ate her McDonalds ice cream cone,
the 69-cent vanilla of it.

How she pointed her tongue
to take tiny licks,
dwindled the swirled

hill into a plateau,
then a ground cave.
How she carefully

peeled the wrapper
from her cone
while mine lay flat,

emptied in two minutes.
How I'd forgotten to notice
the texture and sweetness.

How she crunched her cone
in slow motion mini-bites,
relishing, relishing,

her eyes a clear blue,
fringed in lashes thicker
than mine covered in mascara.

Food Bank

After praying to my dead friend Jamelle,
asking her to look for him, look after him,
wherever he was. After searching strangers'
faces for his for over a year, he resurfaces,
altered. After he found in a black sack
in his dad's garage, the book, *Message*
to a Troubled World, channeled by my great
grandmother through an Ouija board in the 1940s.
After the methadone clinic. After looking for a church.
After handing water bottles to those holding cardboard
signs at street corners. After scavenging backpacks
from bulk trash, gifting them to those he met along the canals,
those who carried their belongings in plastic bags, he now stands
in a place where he tells me he's never been this happy, serving others.
The answer. This room stacked with milk crates and boxes with graphics
of bananas, metal shelves piled high with iceberg, red bell peppers,
striped melons, cukes and squash, row upon row of Kashi, Kraft Mac
and Cheese, Campbell's cans, jars of Skippy and grape jam. Volunteers
clad in khaki pants and *Pure Heart* T-shirts, arms and legs in wheel-like
motion, food to box, box to the next arms in a line that forms outside the door.
My son grinning, his open hand sweeping the room, pointing to produce,
day-old pastries, dairy, meat, eggs in the walk-in fridge, beams of Tuesday
sunlight scattering through the glass, his face and eyes wide, effervescent, lit.

Acknowledgments

Grateful acknowledgment is made to the following publications, where versions of these pieces have appeared or are forthcoming.

"Alex's Teeth" — *Pact Press: Howling Up to the Sky, New Verse News*

"After the Divorce" — *dancing girl press*

"Ash" — *Grief Becomes You Anthology*

"Bagged" — *Boston Literary Magazine*

"Bless the Bee" — *Mom Egg Review*

"Burning Coal" — *Anti-Heroin Chic*

"Chicken" — *New Verse News, Pact Press Howling Up to the Sky: Opioid Epidemic Anthology*

"Even Bodhisattvas Get the Blues" — *dancing girl press*

"Food Bank" — *Anti-Heroin Chic*

"Hoarding Light" — *New Verse News*

"How to Celebrate Your Daughter's 33rd Birthday When There's No Going Back" — *Rattle*

"I Come from a Line of Women" — *Nasty Women Poets, dancing girl*

"I Dream of Him Somersaulting Underwater" — *Anti-Heroin Chic*

"My Son No Longer Missing" — *Rattle*

"Rise and Fall" — *Write Bloody*

"Sonogram"   *Mom Egg Review*

"Why I Go to Al-Anon"   *Anti-Heroin Chic"*

Lines from "One Thing You Should Know About Protecting Your Kids," originally published at *Role Reboot,* appear in *Blame It on the Serpent* as section breaks.

About the Author

Susan Vespoli lives in Phoenix, Arizona, where she relies on the power of writing to stay sane. She's taught Montessori preschoolers and ENG101 to community college students, owned a school, delivered newspapers, bicycled up a mountain, rehabbed a few extreme fixer-upper houses, and currently facilitates virtual writing circles on writers.com. Her work has been published in *Rattle, Mom Egg Review, NASTY WOMEN POETS: An Unapologetic Anthology of Subversive Verse, Nailed Magazine*, and other cool spots. For more, check out her website at https://susanvespoli.com/

CPSIA information can be obtained
at www.ICGtesting.com
Printed in the USA
LVHW032109010222
709519LV00002B/109

"I seek out poetry for solace, for connection, and this is just what I found in Susan Vespoli's *Blame It on the Serpent*. The poems are sharp, direct, unflinching. Vespoli invites us in as her companions as she charts a difficult journey and faces her own agency as a woman and mother."

—**Debra Gwartney**, author of *Live Through This: A Mother's Memoir of Runaway Daughters* and *I Am a Stranger Here Myself.*

"*Blame It on the Serpent* is a 3am wellness check on the loved ones who break your heart. **Susan Vespoli** sifts through Ziploc bags, Zigzag papers, and scorched tinfoil to confront the opioid addiction that kidnapped her children, as teeth and marriage disintegrate. Vespoli's lines pull unconditional beauty from the wreckage of each page to accept the things she cannot change, but accept it slant. Vespoli writes the most vulnerable over-the-counter poems you can get without a prescription."

—**Shawnte Orion**, author of *Gravity & Spectacle*

Susan Vespoli lives in Phoenix, Arizona where she relies on the power of writing to stay sane. She's taught Montessori preschoolers and ENG101 to community college students, owned a school, delivered newspapers, bicycled up a mountain, rehabbed a few extreme fixer-upper houses, and currently facilitates virtual writing circles on writers.com. Her work has been published in *Rattle, Mom Egg Review, NASTY WOMEN POETS: An Unapologetic Anthology of Subversive Verse, Nailed Magazine,* and other cool spots. For more, check out her website at https://susanvespoli.com/

$19.99 / POETRY

www.finishinglinepress.com

ISBN 978-1-64662-732-5

9 781646 627325

51999

Changes in Transportation

by Barbara Wood

This book is about transportation. You will read about many different ways to travel. You will also learn about how transportation has changed over time.

Vocabulary

invention

engine

vehicle

ISBN: 0-328-14806-7

5 6 7 8 9 10 V0G1 14 13 12 11 10 09 08 07 06